**ANCHOR BOOKS**

THERE ONCE WAS . . .

Edited by

Simon Harwin

First published in Great Britain in 2003 by
ANCHOR BOOKS
Remus House,
Coltsfoot Drive,
Peterborough, PE2 9JX
Telephone (01733) 898102

All Rights Reserved

Copyright Contributors 2003

SB ISBN 1 84418 242 8

FOREWORD

Anchor Books is a small press, established in 1992, with the aim of promoting readable poetry to as wide an audience as possible.

We hope to establish an outlet for writers of poetry who may have struggled to see their work in print.

The poems presented here have been selected from many entries, and as always editing proved to be a difficult task.

I trust this selection will delight and please the authors and all those who enjoy reading poetry.

Simon Harwin
Editor

CONTENTS

LIMERICK

There once was a parson from Peel
Who insisted on chips with each meal
But, sadly, one day
He attempted to pray
And found he was too fat to kneel.

Alan Millard

SHAGGY SPAGGI

There was an old lady called Betty
Who had hair like half-cooked spaghetti,
As it often looked matted
I suggested she plait it
And tie up her boat in the jetty!

Janet Anne Lowther

THINGS TO DO ON YOUR BIRTHDAY

Drink a bottle or two of champagne,
Sing a song; wear a thong; fly to Spain,
Paint the town red,
Eat biscuits in bed,
It's a year 'til it comes round again!

Jane Seabourne

BUSH WHACK

Laura says that he's easy to love,
When he speaks - simple to make fun of.
Best support his attack,
On Saddam and Iraq,
Friends are allies, when Bush comes to shove.

Lorri Benedik

LIMERICK

There was a young lady of Tring
Who went out one night on a fling
When asked to be naughty
By a man over forty
Sighed, 'No, I can't do such a thing.'

P French

THERE WAS A YOUNG . . .

There was a young film buff called Bain,
Whose favourite film star was John Wayne.
He was fond of 'True Grit'
Which is obviously s**t,
But he watched it again and again.

Robert Kennedy

A DONE DEED POET

McGonagall came from Dundee
And a terrible poet was he
Sold bad verse on the street
At one penny per sheet
But he still made more money than me

Ron Beaumont

LIMERICK

There was a young athlete from Wales
Who enjoyed the taste of snails
As they were ten a penny
She ate very many
And now when racing she always fails

Colin Jones

KO . . . OK?

There once was a limerick writer
Who was known as a fabulous fighter
She could knock up a song
While she knocked out King Kong
And she weighed in at six stone - or *lighter!*

D M Anderson

UNTITLED

A modernist poet called Dan
Wrote lines that didn't quite scan,
He became all the rage,
The toast of the age,
Two-timing, non-rhyming top man.

Jack Scrafton

NOAH'S GRUMBLES

Said Noah, when building the ark,
'I'll be glad when we've done with this lark.
For the woodworms and moles
Keep on making such holes,
We'll be lucky to finish by dark.'

Margaret B Baguley

HOMELESS JACK

There was a young boy called Jack
Who carried all he owned on his back
He fell asleep one night
Was robbed by daylight
And now he lives in a sack.

Rita Pulford

LIMERICK

A gentle young lady called Jill
Was in love with a man named Bill
But Bill didn't know
Jill loved him, and so
He got married, the bride's name was Lill.

Joan Gray

UNTITLED

There was an old man named Davey
He had spent all his life in the Navy
His sister, if we mention her, was a Chelsea pensioner
Her name was Dan but she wasn't a man
And the only boat she used was for gravy.

Vann Scytere

UNTITLED

There was an old man on a roof
Whose manner was most uncouth
The neighbours disliked him
One threatened to fight him
And now he is minus a tooth.

Dorothy Holloway

THE HUNGRY PUNTER

A man called Raymond from Pinner
Put his money on a 'dead cert' winner
At the end of the course
Oh! Where was the horse?
Poor Ray couldn't afford any dinner!

G D Furse

LIMERICK

A young lady named Rosy McAll
Won first prize at a fancy dress ball,
Would you Adam and Eve it?
You would never believe it,
She was wearing a fig leaf, that's all.

Roy Dickinson

TOM BLAND

A young airline pilot, Tom Bland
Had trouble when trying to land
He'd take off all right
Could handle the flight
But rarely came down where he planned.

Daniel Jack

CREAM ANYONE?

A well-noted chef on the telly
Was blessed with a gigantic belly
He flambe'd with rum
Set fire to his tum
And that's when his knees turned to jelly!

Margaret A Mattinson

LIMERICK

A host of invaders from Mars
Came to Earth with a shipment of stars,
But the people of Woking
Declared they were joking
And had them all put behind bars.

Martin Winbolt-Lewis

THE BIG SNEEZE

There was a young lady called Jenny
Whose sneezes were frequent and many
They were also so loud
That they drew a crowd
From Aberdeen to Abergevenny.

Joyce Walker

LIMERICK

There was a shepherd called Bill
Who kept sheep up on the hill,
One day in the fog
He fell in a bog
And his sheep are looking for him still.

Lynn Mottram

MAN OF KENT

There was a young man of Kent
Whose legs were truly bent
But much to his cost
His feet were so lost
His knees knocked a hole in his tent

Juliana Moon

HARRY LIMERICK

A young wizard called Harry Potter
Attends Hogwarts with a wand not a jotter,
They put his powers to the test
To make him the best,
Harry's number 1 against any evil plotter.

Anne Sackey

LIMERICK

There was a young man from Kildair
Who had a whirlwind affair,
He made love in the high street,
He made love in the bushes
He made love on the park bench in front of his Mrs.

R Law

LIMERICK

There was a young 'Aussie' from Sydney
Who developed a liking for kidney,
And liver and tripe
Which gave him the gripe
He became 'offal' sick then did'ne?

Laura P Williams

STEADY NOW!

A man who was drunk on the street
Found it hard to stand on his feet
He said, 'If I try
To focus my eye
I will surely find some sort of seat.'

Cyril Joyce

UNTITLED

There once was a lady from Peckham
Who followed our David Beckham,
She put on her specs
And ogled his pecs
And if anyone booed him, she'd deck 'em.

Phyllis Spooner

ROTTEN BROTHERS

Something my sister complained was so rotten,
Her name on a sign, once seen not forgotten,
We drove past the place,
Priceless look on her face
When we read it out loud, 'Six Mile Bottom.'

John Peverill

ANTI-CLIMAX

There was a young boxer named Witter,
Reputed to be a big hitter.
He fell to the ground
In one single round,
And all he could hear was birds twitter.

Paul Kelly

DAISY'S LIMERICK

I know a young lady called Daisy,
Her lifestyle is driving me crazy.
She said with a grin,
I've drunk too much gin,
No wonder my memory's hazy!

Rosemary Davies

BRIDE

There stood the bride-to-be,
Supposed to marry at three.
Stood at the altar
The groom had forgot her
And everyone could see!

Laura Squibb

THE PET TIGER FROM SOMERSET

There was an old lady from Somerset
Who purchased a tiger cub as a pet,
But as the tiger got older,
It suddenly got much bolder,
And the lady from Somerset got ate!

Gilly Croft

LIMERICKS

There was a young man from Bombay
Who ordered a meal on a tray
He ate a hot curry
Ran home in a hurry
And sat on the toilet all day.

Terence Leslie

UNTITLED

My girlfriend, Samantha, from Crewe,
Caught a particularly virulent flu,
It turned out to be SARS
So through plate-glass and bars
I kissed her, and found someone new.

Pete Ardern

PEG LEG

There was a young lady named Peg,
Who had a very fine leg,
A glimpse of her thigh
Would cause men to sigh:
'That's better then meat and two veg.'

Ken Cox

TITUS ANDRONICUS

Titus Andronicus was a noted battle winner
and Queen Tamora was a very bad sinner.
Limbs were removed
and treachery proved,
then Tamora ate her two sons for dinner.

Andrew Banks

CUISINE

There was a young lady from Norwich
Who dined on burnt toast and cold porridge
One day with a hiss
She said, 'I'm fed up with this!'
And signed on at a catering college.

Richard Youngs

LIMERICK

Rabbie Burns, a lad was he
He had no drugs
Nor met thugs in pubs
He knew a thing or two
Between me and you
The rushes were green
Tho' seldom seen
His eyes only for Jean

Mary Hudson

LIMERICK

A lady living on the equator
Was teasing a large alligator
She hit it hard on the nose
Which made it mad I suppose
For it opened its mouth and it ate her.

Thomas R Slater

BIG BEN

There was a young man named Ben
Who rang people's bells now and then
When the people got mad
And said Ben was so bad
He just laughed and rang them again.

Joan Briggs

UNTITLED

There was a young lass from Ipswich
Who had an uncontrollable twitch
On the day of her marriage
She drove her own carriage
Ending rear upward in a ditch.

Alan Seaward

LIMERICK

There was a young man called Mike
Who wanted to ride his new bike
But when he got on
Found his balance was gone
So he thought he'd do better to hike

Lynda Long

UNTITLED

There was a young lady from Clare,
Who taught her young pupils with care,
She took them on trips
To see museums and ships,
Then staggered home much worse for wear.

Joan Hammond

DIVING DIVA

One night in the Royal Albert Hall,
a famous soprano did fall
in the orchestra pit.
Though she didn't quite fit,
she knocked 'em all dead, wall to wall!

Kathryn Newbrook

LIMERICK

There was a little woman from Chisleholme
Who fell into a bucket of thick, gooey red foam
She flapped all about
Till she was pulled out
But sadly was mistaken for a garden gnome.

Octavia Hornby

UNTITLED

There was a young lady in blue,
Who tried on a new matching shoe.
She bent over in haste
To tie up the lace,
And split her fine dress near' in two.

Diane Pointer

UNTITLED

There once was a fairy called Lill
    Who made love every night wily-nil
Then some words from her doc
    Gave her quite a shock
Now she wished she had stayed on the pill.

Derek J Morgan

UNTITLED

A mermaid who came from Kinsale
Fell deeply in love with a whale
The whale in his ardour
Added her to his larder
And swallowed her down to her tail.

Caroline Isherwood

WOAD

Tired old reruns of 'My Friend Flikka'
had so taken the eye of Boedikka,
that the blades on her chariot
chewed up her friend Harriet,
thereby making the roadway much slicka.

Jim Rogerson

LIMERICK

There was an old whore from Cahor
whose house had a wide open door,
so in strolled a horse
she said, 'Straight intercourse?'
He said, 'Neigh, I'm just here for some straw.'

Norman Meadows

UNTITLED

A young lion tamer from Devon
Had big cats the number of seven
One day in a cage
They got in a rage
Now he tames lions in Heaven.

Karen Swan

JACUZZI JAPES

Florrie's a bit of a floosie,
Men? She's really not choosy
But she loves to play hooky
And gets all her nooky
As she wallows in her neighbour's Jacuzzi!

Pamela Carder

UNTITLED

There was a young lass from Australia,
Whose nose was shaped like a dahlia!
Two pence a smell
Was all very well,
But three pence a pick was a failure!

W Oliver

LITTLE WET DOG

There was a small puppy named Cuddles
Who ran out and paddled in puddles,
They washed him quite roughly
And said, 'That's enoughly!'
Now Cuddles won't paddle in puddles.

Margaret Ballard

LIMERICK

A man asked a lady ship builder
If she'd build one for three thousand gilder
But when she'd finished the boat
It just wouldn't float
So he pulled out his shot gun and killed her.

Dorothy Kemp

BAD CAKE

There was an old man from Long Eaton
Who would give his wife a good beating
For nothing at all,
One day she'll stand tall
And see the bad cake she's been eating.

Donna Matheson

A LIMERICK

The Titanic will never sink
That's what its makers did think
But the lifeboats though plenty
Went down nearly empty
And most people ended up in the drink!

Rowena Haley

A DOGGY LIMERICK

While walking the sands at Pendine,
A whippet-cross stood on a mine,
As he went on his way,
I heard a Voice say -
'The racing in Heaven is fine!'

Jo Brookes

ONLY THE BEST

There was a young woman of twenty,
Who had suitors a plenty,
But she wouldn't part,
With her little heart,
For anyone other than gentry.

Patricia Dixon MacArthur

LIMERICKS

The Sound Of Music

A short, fat pressman named Morgan
Had just a very tiny organ,
He told his girlfriend with a grin
It's very hard when I begin
But it's music, oft' Recorden.

Nursery Rhyme

Old Mother Hubbard
She went to the cupboard
To quench her poor lodger's thirst.
When she got there
The cupboard was bare
Her husband had been there first.

Gordon P Charkin

LIMERICKS

There was a young man from Carstairs
Whose feet to dead horses were compared
When he took off a sock
Most went into shock
And took a deep breath if they dared.

There was once a gardener from Leeds
Who was accused of going to seed
He said, 'I'm still hale and hearty
So cut out the malarkey
You are just a shower of weeds.'

James Rodger

LIMERICK

A gardening lady of Kew
Spoke psalms to the trees that she grew
To one wilting tree
She said, 'Psalm 23
Is the one I'm reciting to Yew!'

Ivan S Thomas

TOMMY

A Scot who lived in the heather
One day was under the weather,
So into his tam
He poured a wee dram,
How's that for a wee bit of blather.

Julia Amos

UNTITLED

A good limerick should have no confusion,
Theme and story must have a correct fusion.
Rhyme and rhythm must be right
And the punch line, have bite,
To bring the whole to a satisfactory conclusion.

Marian Roach

UNTITLED

There once was a clown from a circus
Who ran off and joined up with the Ghurkas
They asked, 'Can you cook?'
He replied, 'Take a look
At my custard pies which are just first class.'

John Black

HOW NOT TO CURRY FAVOUR

The hanky in your hand was sodden
Nap on the flock looked down-trodden
Our carafe of house red
Was empty and dead
And the look you gave me an odd 'un

The waiter had noted your tears
As he brought to our table some beers
In an atmosphere cold
Pregnant pause growing old
Next table had pinned back its ears

Black mascara ran down your cheek
As if your dark eyes sprung a leak
With a lager us each
Compromise tried to reach
But no one prepared yet to speak

Why had your mood once buoyant turned grim
I'd said in that dress you looked slim
Perchance that remark
I'd only said for a lark
Miss Piggy you'll soon need the gym

I R Finch

MMMM CHOCOLATES

A lovely young lady called Vicky
found chocolates decidedly tricky.
When she soaked in the tub
to have a good scrub
those sweets all became very sticky.

The chocolates got eaten away
and her tum just got bigger each day.
But though chocs harmed her tum
they were great for her bum!
It's perfect, what more can I say?

D G W Garde

THESPIAN LIMERICKS

A Shakespearean actor named Mott,
Didn't care for his role, not a jot,
Learned his lines very slow,
By the night of the show,
He'd forgotten the whole bloody lot!

At Hamlet he once had a bash,
Of Macbeth he did make a right hash,
When he played Romeo,
He messed up the show,
From the balcony, fell with a crash.

While doing 'Taming of the Shrew',
His memory cells were too few,
When he stuttered and dried,
The producer just cried,
'I thought that all your lines you knew!'

When the company tried the tempest,
They thought that this would be their best,
Poor Mott thought he knew it,
But once more he blew it,
The audience wasn't impressed!

He gave up on Shakespeare in time,
And tried his hand at pantomime,
It was easier and better,
For a serial forgetter,
When each second line was a rhyme.

He was offered a part 'Tour de Force',
So he said, 'I'll accept it of course,'
He then found his forte,
Having nothing to say,
As the arse of a pantomime horse!

Mick Nash

LIMITATION

With a single poem in limerick
And total five lines to be in it
There is taste without backing
One crisp from the packing
Upholding the rules and the limit.

Reg C H Baggs

JOLLY JACK

There was a young poet called Jack
Unemployed because of the sack
Cos he spent all day
Thinking of what to say
So his work would get published not sent back

A small firm called Anchor said yes
We will publish, oh God bless
Fame if not fortune is his at last
He's off to celebrate and have a blast
The future is good so forget the past

So now he spends his time
Finding thoughts and words to rhyme
It's jolly good fun, a bit of a laugh
He never stops thinking in the bus or the bath
And why not, it's no crime
And our hero is now in his prime

Jack Couch

UNTITLED

Two lovers, one tandem, a storm,
A barn . . . dark, cosy and warm,
When rain had stopped,
Their shorts, somehow, swapped,
. . . But I guess that you know the form.

David Kellard

MONA

Crack, crack, crack go my knees
I sniffle and I wheeze
Not so very long ago I could clamber up the trees
My bosom now is flat and my shoulders very round
Please God, grant my feet stay safely on the ground.

Peggy Johnson

OBESITY

A gourmet with taste so consummate
Would gorge on his food so exquisite
But, sad to relate
He got in a bad state
By his excess of sodium glutamate.

Patrick Brady

THE SAILOR

There once was a sailor from Diss
Who met a pretty young miss
He fell for her charms
Near Berney Arms
Contented the sailor from Diss.

Steve Glason

AN ODIUM OF PODIUM

The problem I think with concerto
It does, don't you know, just go on so
It can be quite loud
And too often allowed
To be too much forte crescendo.

Martin Harris Parry

LIMERICK

There was a young kitten called Moses,
Who had an abundance of 'toeses'.
'I've got that amount
'Cos my mum can't count,'
He purrs as he winks, as he dozes.

Stephanie Stone

THE DO-IT-YOURSELF LORD

There once was a man named Landseer,
Who decided to apply to become a peer.
He sent off his testimonial -
Designed a crest ceremonial
But when he arrived was no nearer to being a Lord than a Court jester.

R Wiltshire

IS IT ME?

Is it me, am I really so bad?
Do I really make people feel sad?
Does my temper and mood
make me so far from good,
could I not make someone feel glad?

Is it me, am I really so blue?
Are my kind days really so few?
I mean to be nice
like sugar and spice,
is it too late to change, start anew?

Is it me, am I really so bold?
Do I really blow hot and cold?
I should bite my tongue
I'm no longer young,
do I really have to grow old?

Ann Odger

POEM

To write a poem I thought would be easy
But every word I wrote sounded so cheesy
Try as I might I just couldn't get it right
It sounded good in my head
But I may as well have stayed in bed
Pen to paper would not rhyme
All I did was waste my time
To have a talent must be great
But I guess I'll just have to wait
But after all is said and done
I think I've gone and written one.

Maureen Morris

FROM READING

There was a young lady of Reading
who heard it exclaimed at a wedding,
'I thought he was gay
but she's in the way -
so he must have crumpled her bedding.'

Owen Edwards

UNTITLED

There was a young woman called Molly
Who sat down on a sprig of holly.
She howled in great pain
As it started to rain
And cried, 'To make it worse, I've forgotten my brolly.'

Molly M Hamilton

LIAR

I know a cowardly lying b*****d,
Telling the truth he hasn't yet mastered.
Lies pour from his mouth and nose,
Even where his water flows,
Which always leaves me flabbergasted!

Carol Ann Darling

LIMERICKS FOR GERIATRICS

A group of young male geriatrics
Went out one day seeking kicks
They met a few dames
Who wouldn't give their names
'Cos the geriatrics could only give cat licks.

Eric Allday

SICKLY SAILOR

There once was a young sailor
Who went to sea on a whaler,
When he came back to dry land
He found he couldn't stand
And his countenance was twenty shades paler.

E D Bowen

THE OLD WOMAN

There was an old woman who lived by the sea
She sat in her chair and drank cups of tea
When the tide came in
She retired to her bed
And stared out the window at the moon instead
One day she floated way up high
Her spirit was drawn by a light in the sky
She couldn't make herself any tea
She couldn't sit by the sea
But she could float beside the stars
And go to planets like Venus and Mars.

Tina Davis

SCHOOL ASSEMBLY

Said the head, trying his students to shock,
As he gave his assembly short talk,
'I am rather afraid
That like sheep you have strayed
Now I feel I am the shepherd of the flock.'

Up spoke a young student named Taff
'Sir, your metaphors may cause a laugh,
But in the same context can be said,
Your deputy head
Is the little crook at the top of your staff!'

Norrie Ferguson

FIFTEENTH CENTURY HISTORY

The War of the Roses were fought
Very fiercely: the middle age court
Simply could not decide
If the odd regicide
Was a good or a terrible thought.

Helen Marsh Jeffries

UNTITLED

Young Shakespeare, his friends call him Will,
Was quite a dab hand with the quill.
Wrote great dramas in verse,
But what seems so perverse,
They're trying to decipher them still.

Jean Kelly

DEUCE!

There once was a girl from Porthcawl
Who loved tennis, had bats, but no ball!
Whilst out on the courts, she fell on the lawn
And laying there, her dress, all ragged and torn
Was pleased to find it was men's doubles!

Maureen Westwood-O'Hara

TOP SECRET

'I don't care if those weapons aren't there,'
said a vain politician called Blair.
'I'd be much more concerned
if the populace learned
that I'm rapidly losing my hair!'

Frank Dunnill

THE HAND OF FATE

There was a young man called Reidy
Who was terribly, terribly greedy
He bit off his thumb
Whilst eating a plum
And now he is one of the needy.

Patrick Morrissey

BECALMED

An intrepid sailor called Peare
Found a woman who knew how to steer
She taught him the ropes
And hoisted his hopes
When Peare met his peer at the pier

Marion Evans

LIMERICK

There was a young lady from Taunton
Who bought a young horse for dancing
It brought out the sun
The race it did win
And it ended with Cavalier prancing.

Nicola Barnes

No Comfort

I've had it all, up to here and more,
When we are in bed, I hear your snore,
In the time that comes with hense,
I do become myself very tense,
Did always bother me, somewhat before.

Where can I fathom a sleep to the fore,
Your snores, through the night, have made me sore.
That mouth open wide, I've no recompense,
I've had it all.

I'm lying here, awake and deplore,
That sound right through me, unto the core,
Does make of my headache, not of sense,
There's your whistle, a grunt, non relents,
You sicken me now, becomes a chore,
I've had it all.

Hugh Campbell

WE WILL MEET AGAIN

We will meet again I truly believe
The friends and the family for whom we all grieve
To meet and embrace long lost memories recall
Forgetting all pain and what did befall
Contented to be in the arms that did leave.

To blissfully lose all our troubles and pain
Surrounded by loved ones rejoice once again
Sweet surrender in your true lover's arms
We will meet again.

When climbing the stairs the gates open wide
The family all smiling and waiting inside
Into welcome arms the love you so missed
The long for remembered warmth of his kiss
Contented to be once again by their side
We will meet again.

K Townsley

ANCHOR BOOKS
SUBMISSIONS INVITED
SOMETHING FOR EVERYONE

ANCHOR BOOKS GEN - Any subject,
light-hearted clean fun, nothing unprintable
please.

THE OPPOSITE SEX - Have your say on the
opposite gender. Do they drive you mad or can
we co-exist in harmony?

THE NATURAL WORLD - Are we destroying
the world around us? What should we do to
preserve the beauty and the future of our planet -
you decide!

All poems no longer than 30 lines.
Always welcome! No fee!
Plus cash prizes to be won!

Mark your envelope (eg *The Natural World)*
And send to:
Anchor Books
Remus House, Coltsfoot Drive
Peterborough, PE2 9JX

OVER £10,000 IN POETRY PRIZES
TO BE WON!

Send an SAE for details on our latest
competition!